CW01647095

Who Is He that Overcometh the World?

Dag Heward-Mills

Parchment House

Unless otherwise stated, all Scripture quotations are taken from the King James Version of the Bible.

Who Is He that Overcometh the World?

Copyright © 2022 Dag Heward-Mills

Published by Parchment House 2022
1st Printing 2022

Find out more about Dag Heward-Mills
Healing Jesus Campaign
Write to: evangelist@daghewardmills.org
Website: www.daghewardmills.org
Facebook: Dag Heward-Mills
Twitter: @EvangelistDag

ISBN: 978-1-64330-528-8

All rights reserved under international copyright law.
Written permission must be secured from the publisher to use or reproduce any part of this book.

Contents

CHAPTER 1

Who Overcomes the World?

WHO IS HE THAT OVERCOMETH THE WORLD, but he that believeth that Jesus is the Son of God?

1 John 5:5

The scripture above is very clear that the world is something to be overcome. Why must we overcome the world? What is the world? I thought the world was a place. I thought the world was this earth that God has created. Why would I need to overcome the earth?

You are asking these questions because you do not understand what exactly the world is. Indeed, the world is a place where we live but the world is much more than that. If the world were simply this earth, there would not be much more to overcome than to ensure that we do not drown in the river or the ocean, or to ensure that we do not fall off a tall tree.

In this book, I want to show you that the world is made up of the physical place we live in *plus* all the other creatures that inhabit this space. *The world is actually a combination of the place, the people and the spirits on the earth and that makes up a very evil world indeed.*

The scripture declares clearly that the whole world lies in wickedness (1 John 5:19). *The world we live in is soaked in evil and this evil environment is what you and I have been born into.*

You are never likely to see the devil himself. You are also not likely to see a demon in your lifetime. However, the presence of these evil spirits creates a strong negative and wicked environment on earth. An evil spirit causes the environment and the disposition of a place to change drastically.

Indeed, you are also not likely to meet most of the wicked people like the murderers, mass killers, rapists, paedophiles, serial killers and other wicked monsters that live on the earth. However, their presence on this earth creates an evil aura and also creates a negative pressure against every good thing on the earth.

The combination of the wilderness environment, the evil spirits and the evil men creates the very wicked world we live in today. This wicked world creates a strong pressure against a believer. It is this strong pressure that we must overcome. That is why scripture says, "Who is he that has overcome the world?" Only someone who believes in Jesus can overcome the evil pressures and influences that are present in our world today.

Indeed, this world is not our home! It is a place God has brought us to for a reason.

Let us look at the components of the world we live in. Let us understand the different components of the world that generate so much pressure against believers. As you read this book, you will understand why this world can never be your home.

1. THE WORLD IS A PHYSICALLY DANGEROUS PLACE.

They that see thee shall narrowly look upon thee, and consider thee, saying, Is this the man that made the earth to tremble, that did shake kingdoms; THAT MADE THE WORLD AS A WILDERNESS, and destroyed the cities thereof; that opened not the house of his prisoners?

Isaiah 14:16-17

The world is a *physically dangerous place* that is described in the Bible. Isaiah tells us that the beautiful world that God created has been converted into a wilderness. A wilderness is a wild and uninhabited area, left in a state of disfavour and bewildering confusion. The world that God created was a beautiful place.

He hath made every thing beautiful in his time: also he hath set the world in their heart, so that no man can find out the work that God maketh from the beginning to the end.

Ecclesiastes 3:11

And God saw every thing that he had made, and, behold, it was very good. And the evening and the morning were the sixth day.

Genesis 1:31

The beautiful world that God created is no longer as it was when it was first created. Isaiah stated clearly that it had been turned into a wilderness. Our world today is full of many dangers. Many things in this world can end the life of a human being. Wild animals, snakes, wild fires, drought, excessive heat, excessive cold, floods, earthquakes, volcanoes and so on regularly destroy human life. The world we live in is filled with dangerous rivers and oceans that drown men. The world we live in is full of viruses, bacteria and parasites that kill human beings. The world we live in is full of wild animals that kill men all the time. This world has become a dangerous place.

God did not create a world that would attack and eat up its inhabitants. Human beings used to live for as long as a thousand years. Obviously, something has happened to God's beautiful creation. Isaiah tells us that satan turned it into a wilderness. The world now attacks its inhabitants and largely wipes them out by the age of seventy or eighty.

The world we know replaced another older world that was destroyed. Since this world has been destroyed by the presence of evil spirits and evil men, it will have to be replaced by another world.

> For if God spared not the angels that sinned, but cast them down to hell, and delivered them into chains of darkness, to be reserved unto judgment; AND SPARED NOT THE OLD WORLD, BUT SAVED NOAH THE EIGHTH PERSON, a preacher of righteousness, bringing in the flood upon the world of the ungodly;
>
> 2 Peter 2:4-5

> For this they willingly are ignorant of, that by the word of God the heavens were of old, and the earth standing out of the water and in the water: WHEREBY THE WORLD THAT THEN WAS, BEING OVERFLOWED WITH WATER, PERISHED:
>
> 2 Peter 3:5-6

It is important to note that the world that we know as our home is only one of the worlds that exist today. I know you think that we are the centre of the universe. But you can see from the planets and the stars that there is much more out there.

> Hath in these last days spoken unto us by his Son, whom he hath appointed heir of all things, BY WHOM ALSO HE MADE THE WORLDS;
>
> Hebrews 1:2

> THROUGH FAITH WE UNDERSTAND THAT THE WORLDS WERE FRAMED BY THE WORD OF GOD, so that things which are seen were not made of things which do appear.
>
> Hebrews 11:3

2. THE WORLD IS A PLACE FULL OF WICKED PEOPLE.

> **And we know that we are of God, and the whole world lieth in wickedness.**
>
> **1 John 5:19**

The world is also made up of wicked people. These wicked people have changed this world into a terrible hellhole. I once spoke to a prisoner about his experience in prison. He described a terrible time when he was in a room with eight other men, some of whom were murderers.

He said violent fights would break out at any time and anyone could get hurt. He lived for three years in a room with these convicted murderers. He lived in fear and fright every day of his life whilst in prison. Being in the company of violent men, murderers, rapists, paedophiles and serial killers is not an easy thing. You would be under great pressure in the prison because violence and murder could occur at any time.

Indeed, it is the company you have in a place that either makes it enjoyable or horrible. Dear friend, the company you have with you at any time makes all the difference. In this world, you are forced to live in the company of wicked people. Let us have a look at the list of people who create the evil pressure in the world.

a. A world of evil people.

> Who gave himself for our sins, that he might deliver us from THIS PRESENT EVIL WORLD, according to the will of God and our Father:
>
> Galatians 1:4

b. A world of sinful people.

> And he is the propitiation for our sins: and not for ours only, but also for THE SINS OF THE WHOLE WORLD.
>
> 1 John 2:2

c. A world of lustful people.

> For ALL THAT IS IN THE WORLD, THE LUST of the flesh, and THE LUST of the eyes, and the pride of life, is not of the Father, but is of the world.
>
> 1 John 2:16

d. A world of anti-Christ people.

> Hereby know ye the Spirit of God: Every spirit that confesseth that Jesus Christ is come in the flesh is of God:
>
> And every spirit that confesseth not that Jesus Christ is come in the flesh is not of God: and THIS IS THAT SPIRIT OF ANTICHRIST, WHEREOF YE HAVE HEARD THAT IT SHOULD COME; AND EVEN NOW ALREADY IS IT IN THE WORLD.
>
> 1 John 4:2-3

The people of this world are anti-church, anti-God, anti-pastors, anti-man of God and anti-Christ. Never think that the world loves you. Never think that the world will ever like you.

The world puts up with you because it cannot eliminate you totally. Through a series of hidden underground moves, you will sooner or later feel the animosity, hatred and antagonism that exist against God and the people of God.

e. A world of liars.

> For MANY DECEIVERS ARE ENTERED INTO THE WORLD, who confess not that Jesus Christ is come in the flesh. This is a deceiver and an antichrist.
>
> 2 John 1:7

The people in this world have many deceivers amongst them. One of the biggest characteristics of people in this world is lying. Many people in the world are simply liars. Lying is probably the commonest thing in the world. When God wanted to differentiate Himself from men, He simply said that He was not a liar (Numbers 23:19). The human race is identified by its lying and deception.

f. A world of corrupt men.

> Whereby are given unto us exceeding great and precious promises: that by these ye might be partakers of the divine nature, having escaped THE CORRUPTION THAT IS IN THE WORLD through lust.
>
> 2 Peter 1:4

The people in this world are spoilt, destroyed and corrupt. It is not possible to reverse corruption. You can only slow it down. That is why the world is getting worse with every passing day. The corruption in this world spreads and affects believers. It is this corruption that puts pressure on anyone living on earth to also be corrupt.

3. THE WORLD IS A PLACE FULL OF EVIL SPIRITS.

> **And he cried mightily with a strong voice, saying, Babylon the great is fallen, is fallen, and is become the**

habitation of devils, and the hold of every foul spirit, and a cage of every unclean and hateful bird.

Revelation 18:2

The world is a place full of evil spirits. This world, just like Babylon, is totally destroyed because of the presence of all these evil spirits.

These evil spirits have changed this world into a terrible place of sin and evil. The beautiful world that God created as a home and a paradise for men has been turned into the habitation of devils.

Babylon is one of the cities in this world. Notice how it is described as a fallen, destroyed and desolate place because it was inhabited by evil spirits. Notice how these evil spirits have completely changed the atmosphere in this world.

a. **The prince of the power of the air:** This evil spirit controls the airwaves and atmosphere.

Wherein in time past ye walked according to the course of this world, according to the prince of the power of the air, the spirit that now worketh in the children of disobedience:

Ephesians 2:2

b. **The god of this world:** This evil spirit controls the trends and circumstances in our world.

In whom the god of this world hath blinded the minds of them which believe not, lest the light of the glorious gospel of Christ, who is the image of God, should shine unto them.

2 Corinthians 4:4

c. **The great dragon:** This evil spirit establishes the deceptions in this world.

And the great dragon was cast out, that old serpent, called the Devil, and Satan, which deceiveth the whole world: he was cast out into the earth, and his angels were cast out with him.

Revelation 12:9

d. **The spirit of the world:** This evil spirit controls the people in the world. The people of the world are influenced by the spirit of the world and the people of God are influenced by the Spirit of God!

Now we have received, not THE SPIRIT OF THE WORLD, but the spirit which is of God; that we might know the things that are freely given to us of God.

1 Corinthians 2:12

4. **THE WORLD IS THE CURRENT EVIL SYSTEM.**

In whom the god of this world hath blinded the minds of them which believe not, lest the light of the glorious gospel of Christ, who is the image of God, should shine unto them.

2 Corinthians 4:4

The world is an evil system created by the presence of evil men and evil spirits. It is governed by evil values and beliefs. All Christians are under pressure, once they are in this evil world.

A combination of a fallen and desolate creation, plus the presence of millions of evil spirits, plus the presence of billions of wicked men creates a terrible evil system that is called the "world". Welcome to the world that will present itself as your principal test and challenge as long as you are alive on earth.

All through the Bible, you will find exhortations and instructions to be careful of this world. You will find warnings not to love the world, not to befriend the world and not to be conformed to this evil world.

CHAPTER 2

If This World is Not My Home, What Is It?

As thou hast sent me into the world, even SO HAVE I ALSO SENT THEM INTO THE WORLD. AND FOR THEIR SAKES I SANCTIFY MYSELF, THAT THEY ALSO MIGHT BE SANCTIFIED through the truth. Neither pray I for these alone, but for them also which shall believe on me through their word; That they all may be one; as thou, Father, art in me, and I in thee, that they also may be one in us: that the world may believe that thou hast sent me.

John 17:18-21

We have been sent into this dangerous world to preach the gospel and to win the lost for Jesus Christ. Jesus was sent on this dangerous mission into the world and He lost His life by the age of thirty-three. We have also been sent on a "danger mission" and into this dangerous world. Welcome to your "danger mission"!

1. This world is not your home; it is your harvest field.

> THE FIELD IS THE WORLD; the good seed are the children of the kingdom; but the tares are the children of the wicked one;
>
> Matthew 13:38

This fact, that the world is not your home, must sink deep into your heart. If this world is not your home, then what is it? *This world is your harvest field.* Christians must see the world as what it is. It is the harvest field that God has placed before you. No one tries to settle down in a harvest field and build a house in the midst of the corn and the wheat.

A harvest field is a work place. It is not a place of rest. Nor is it a place of comfort. It is a place of great labour and toil. Get used to the idea that this world is not your home. Get used to the idea that you are living in the midst of your harvest field. Your work is staring at you in the face.

2. This world is not your home; it is your school.

> For the invisible things of him FROM THE CREATION OF THE WORLD ARE CLEARLY SEEN, being understood by the things that are made, even his eternal power and Godhead; so that they are without excuse:
>
> Romans 1:20

> Doth not even NATURE ITSELF TEACH YOU, that, if a man have long hair, it is a shame unto him?
>
> 1 Corinthians 11:14

If this world is not your home, then what is it? This world is a school for you. This world is a place you have come to learn about God. The invisible things of God are understood from the creation of the world. The animals in this world, the plants in this world, the rivers, the seas, the oceans, the mountains and the lakes are all revelations showing the nature of God and His awesomeness. Nature is one of the greatest teachers.

There is no other planet that exists and reveals the greatness of God as much as the earth does.

3. This world is not your home; it is your training and testing ground.

> And thou shalt remember all the way which the LORD thy God led thee these forty years in the wilderness, TO HUMBLE THEE, AND TO PROVE THEE, to know what was in thine heart, whether thou wouldest keep his commandments, or no.
>
> Deuteronomy 8:2

The experiences you have in this world are to train you in many things. Notice how the Lord took the children of Israel through the wilderness for forty years. Forty years in the wilderness was intended to humble and test the children of Israel to see what they were made of and whether they would obey God or not. Every experience you go through is educative. If you have a teachable spirit, you will learn many things from the experiences you have.

> For whom the Lord loveth he chasteneth, and scourgeth every son whom he receiveth. If ye endure chastening, God dealeth with you as with sons; for what son is he whom the father chasteneth not?
>
> Hebrews 12:6-7

The word, "chasten" means to train, to educate and to discipline. In this world, God will chasten you and scourge you like a son. To chasten also means to punish and instruct you. Many experiences you will have in this world are the chastening of the Lord. He is training you, equipping you, educating you and correcting you. God is chastening you whilst you are in this world so that you become a better person.

4. This world is not your home; it is a place to prove that you are an overcomer.

There is a special place for overcomers. There are special rewards for overcomers. There are crowns for overcomers. Those who overcome great challenges, great temptations and great hardships and prevail to bear much fruit for the Lord must know that their works are being taken note of.

In heaven, there will be a special section for overcomers. An overcomer is someone who does not make excuses. An overcomer is someone who goes through every barrier, jumps over every hurdle, crosses every mountain, swims across every river and prevails to overturn the plans of the enemy.

All through the book of Revelation, you will notice the phrase, "he that overcometh".

> He that hath an ear, let him hear what the Spirit saith unto the churches; TO HIM THAT OVERCOMETH will I give to eat of the tree of life, which is in the midst of the paradise of God.
>
> Revelation 2:7

> He that hath an ear, let him hear what the Spirit saith unto the churches; HE THAT OVERCOMETH shall not be hurt of the second death.
>
> Revelation 2:11

> He that hath an ear, let him hear what the Spirit saith unto the churches; TO HIM THAT OVERCOMETH will I give to eat of the hidden manna, and will give him a white stone, and in the stone a new name written, which no man knoweth saving he that receiveth it.
>
> Revelation 2:17

> And HE THAT OVERCOMETH, and keepeth my works unto the end, to him will I give power over the nations:
>
> Revelation 2:26

5. This world is not your home; it is a dangerous wilderness packed with evil spirits and wicked men that you have to overcome.

You must expect to see a lot of wickedness and evil in this world. This world is not your home; it is a wicked place that you must overcome. There is too much evil in the world for it to be a home. There is a lot of wickedness that you will encounter that you must overcome.

> And we know that we are of God, and the whole world lieth in wickedness.
>
> 1 John 5:19

A young person must overcome in this world. Young people are molested, abused and baptised into abominations before they know what is happening to them. The world is full of cruelty, evil, sin, perversions and wickedness. Do not take for granted the kind of place you are in! It can never be your home! It was never intended to be your home! It is a place to prove your ability to overcome!

> That made the world as a wilderness, and destroyed the cities thereof; that opened not the house of his prisoners?
>
> Isaiah 14:17

6. This world is not your home; it is your stage.

> YE ARE THE LIGHT OF THE WORLD. A city that is set on an hill cannot be hid.
>
> Matthew 5:14

> That ye may be blameless and harmless, the sons of God, without rebuke, in the midst of a crooked and perverse

> nation, among whom ye shine as LIGHTS IN THE WORLD;
>
> Philippians 2:15

What happens on stage? That is where you give your best performance. That is where you shine like a star. The stage is where you make yourself known to the audience.

This world is the stage where you will make yourself known to the spirit world and to the eternal world. All of heaven and all of hell will know who you are by the time you finish your performance on the world stage.

You are supposed to shine brightly when you get the chance. This is your chance! You are supposed to shine as lights in the world. Do not attempt to make this world your home. Make this world the stage from where you will shine and throw forth a great light to the world.

Do not fall asleep on the stage. Do not try to make a tent on the stage. Do not try to build a little house on the stage. Just perform your duties and shine for the Lord. You are the light of the world. Your country, your nation, your city, your town, your village is the stage from where you will shine for all men to see your light.

When your time is up you will regret not giving it your best shot. You will regret spending your performing time doing other things. You will regret not acting your best and giving your best performance. Arise and give your best performance of ministry work! Arise and give your best performance of church planting! Arise and give your best performance of missionary work! Arise and give your best performance of evangelism!

This world is the place to shine as a worthy servant, faithful to your mission and to your marching orders. The marching orders are clear: "Go into the world and preach the gospel!" For all eternity, you will be judged, assessed, marked, rewarded or rejected based on these words of Jesus. This world is not a home for you to rest and receive your comforts. This is a place to prove yourself worthy of eternal crowns.

7. **This world is not your home because it cannot compare with what God has planned for you.**

> (OF WHOM THE WORLD WAS NOT WORTHY:) they wandered in deserts, and in mountains, and in dens and caves of the earth.
>
> Hebrews 11:38

This world is greatly inferior to what God has planned for men of faith. In Hebrews, in the great chapter of faith in the Bible, we learn that the faith heroes wandered around in this world, unable to settle down because the world was not worthy of them. Faith people wandered in deserts, in mountains, in dens and caves.

This world is not worthy of your presence. If you are a man of faith, this world is below you! Focus on eternity and the great mansions God has in store for you in eternity.

I once saw a little house that had been built to house the grave of a politician. They were not content to simply mark the grave with a stone. They wanted to mark the grave with a house.

It was a cute little house, about seven metres by ten metres with a special Chinese security door. I marvelled at this little house which human beings had built to house the body of an important man in his village. Indeed, I am sure that God has a better house and mansion for you up in heaven.

CHAPTER 3

Overcome the Pressure to Follow the Course of this World

And you hath he quickened, who were dead in trespasses and sins;

WHEREIN IN TIME PAST YE WALKED ACCORDING TO THE COURSE OF THIS WORLD, according to the prince of the power of the air, the spirit that now worketh in the children of disobedience:

Among whom also we all had our conversation in times past in the lusts of our flesh, fulfilling the desires of the flesh and of the mind; and were by nature the children of wrath, even as others.

Ephesians 2:1-3

It is important to recognize that the world is on a course that is dictated by the devil. The whole world, full of evil men and evil spirits, are rushing down a path laid out for them by satan.

"The course of this world" is the way in which the world goes. The world has a way of going about everything. The worldly course is the way the world goes about achieving things. The worldly way is different from the Christian way. The worldly way is dictated by the prince of the power of the air. These worldly methods of doing things come about because the world's ways are dictated by the god of this world.

1. There is a worldly way to get love and happiness.

There is a worldly progression of relationships. The course of relationships in the world goes down a particular path of deception, immorality and licentiousness. The world only understands this progression of events. Whilst you are living in the world, you will come under pressure to follow the course of the world and live your life with multiple wrong relationships, constant deception, immorality and licentiousness.

2. There is a worldly progression of marriage.

The course of this world towards marriage begins with premarital sex and a full "knowledge" of one another. In the world, people get married to please the society. In the world, people have hundreds of relationships and eventually settle down with one. Most marriages that follow the course of the world follow the course of deception, unfaithfulness, and adultery with prolonged side relationships. It is important that you do everything to escape the course of this world. The course of this world is determined by the prince of the power of the air. The prince of the power of the air dictates this course of events by filling the minds of worldly men and women with secular goals that inspire this lifestyle.

3. There is a worldly way to achieve success.

There is a worldly course to promotion. All worldly achievements are brought about by following the course of this world. The course of this world involves deception, self-aggrandizement, self-enhancement and self-promotion. Vaunting yourself in pride is the course of this world and leads to the destruction that satan so desires to happen to you.

Jesus' method for you to be successful takes a completely different course. Jesus says, humble yourself, go lower, bow down and He will exalt you. But that is not the way of the world. The world wants you to exalt yourself, promote yourself and fight for yourself. Will you follow the dictates of the prince of the power of the air or will you follow the dictates of the Holy Spirit?

4. There is a worldly way to overcome problems.

> Jesus answered, My kingdom is not of this world: IF MY KINGDOM WERE OF THIS WORLD, THEN WOULD MY SERVANTS FIGHT, that I should not be delivered to the Jews: but now is my kingdom not from hence.
>
> John 18:36

There is a worldly way of fighting your battles. There is a worldly way of overcoming and overpowering your enemy. The worldly way is inspired by the flesh and demon activity. In the scripture below, we see the godly way of fighting back. The worldly way to fight is to avenge yourself. The godly way to fight is to leave things to God to exact vengeance on your behalf.

> Dearly beloved, avenge not yourselves, but rather give place unto wrath: for it is written, Vengeance is mine; I will repay, saith the Lord. Therefore if thine enemy hunger, feed him; if he thirst, give him drink: for in so doing thou shalt heap coals of fire on his head. Be not overcome of evil, but overcome evil with good.
>
> Romans 12:19-21

Notice that the worldly way of thinking does not match God's way of thinking. The foolishness of God is wiser than the wisdom of this world.

> For THE WISDOM OF THIS WORLD is foolishness with God. For it is written, He taketh the wise in their own craftiness.
>
> 1 Corinthians 3:19

> But THE WISDOM THAT IS FROM ABOVE is first pure, then peaceable, gentle, and easy to be intreated, full of mercy and good fruits, without partiality, and without hypocrisy.
>
> James 3:17

The people of this world are led by the devil on a particular course. This is called the "course of the world". Many people go along without even knowing that they are on a well-mapped out course that generations have followed mindlessly. They are walking according to the course of this world that is laid out by the prince of the power of the air.

CHAPTER 4

Overcome the Pressure to Conform to this World

And BE NOT CONFORMED TO THIS WORLD: but be ye transformed by the renewing of your mind, that ye may prove what is that good, and acceptable, and perfect, will of God.

Romans 12:2

To be conformed to the world is to yield yourself to the worldly, social and spiritual influences around you. To conform to this world means to comply and to be obedient to this world.

You are not supposed to be compliant and obedient to worldly influences that are trying to change your behaviour. The reason why people conform to this world is so that they can fit in with a group and with the expectations of those around them.

Conformity is simply defined as yielding to group pressures. People conform because they want to be accepted. God does not want you to even desire to be accepted by the world.

1. **Do not be conformed to this world in order to please men.**

> **For do I now persuade men, or God? or DO I SEEK TO PLEASE MEN? for if I yet pleased men, I should not be the servant of Christ.**
>
> **Galatians 1:10**

Paul recognized that he was under pressure to please men, to be accepted by men, to be admired by men and to be recognized by men. Today, there is great pressure to conform to the group called "the world"! You and I are under great pressure to be conformed to the world and to please the world.

Because of this pressure from the world, Christians must actually develop antagonistic attitudes towards the world rather than desiring to be accepted by the world.

What we are actually at war with is the pressure to conform to the world!

Our Christian life is a fight to overcome this pressure to be conformed to this world!

2. Do not be conformed to this world in order to be accepted.

Nevertheless the people refused to obey the voice of Samuel; and they said, Nay; but we will have a king over us; THAT WE ALSO MAY BE LIKE ALL THE NATIONS; and that our king may judge us, and go out before us, and fight our battles.

1 Samuel 8:19-20

You may not be aware of how much pressure you are under to conform to the world system and be accepted. All through the Bible, God is against His people conforming to the world. The Israelites came under great pressure to be just like the nations all around them. Whenever the Israelites conformed to the world, they came under judgment.

You are even under pressure to admire the same things that the world admires. For instance, if you went with friends to a function and a sexually perverted person made a presentation which you found sinful and unacceptable but people around felt was perfectly alright, you might be tempted to conform by pretending to agree with them rather than being the odd one out.

So much happens in the world that we find attractive and we want to be just like the people of this world. Pastors want to be like secular chief executives or presidents. Christians want to be worldly millionaires. Christian musicians want to be worldly stars. Christian citizens want to be rich and famous like every other successful person in the world.

3. Do not be conformed to the way the world speaks.

They are of the world: THEREFORE SPEAK THEY OF THE WORLD, and the world heareth them.

1 John 4:5

The people of this world think in a certain way and speak in a certain way. There is pressure to conform to this world and speak the way the people of this world speak.

The people of this world write words, compose songs and speak in particular characteristic ways. A Christian singer should not be happy if the world likes to listen to his music. If the world likes to listen to the words of your music, it means you are worldly and are of the world. Unfortunately, a lot of Christian music is very conformed to the world. Today, Christian music can be used in nightclubs and the world does not even know that they are dancing to Christian music.

A pastor should not be happy if the world listens or loves to listen to his messages. Worldliness in a pastor causes the world to be attracted to his preaching. Sinners do not enjoy real gospel preaching unless they are getting saved. Sinners are attracted to secularized preaching which sounds like worldly wisdom. Sinners must be attracted to gospel preaching that leads them to salvation through the power of God.

4. Do not conform to the worldly way of thinking:

> **Howbeit we speak wisdom among them that are perfect: YET NOT THE WISDOM OF THIS WORLD, nor of the princes of this world, that come to nought:...**
>
> **Which none of the princes of this world knew: for had they known it, they would not have crucified the Lord of glory.**
>
> **1 Corinthians 2:6, 8**

The wisdom of this world will never be our wisdom. Our wisdom is the word of God. Jesus Himself taught us that a wise man is someone who hears the word of God and obeys it.

Therefore whosoever heareth these sayings of mine, and doeth them, I WILL LIKEN HIM UNTO A WISE MAN, which built his house upon a rock:

Matthew 7:24

You and I have a clear source of wisdom. The word of God is the source of our wisdom. Our wisdom comes from the Holy Scriptures. You must believe that the Bible is the source of wisdom.

And that from a child thou hast known THE HOLY SCRIPTURES, WHICH ARE ABLE TO MAKE THEE WISE unto salvation through faith which is in Christ Jesus.

2 Timothy 3:15

The people of this world have a kind of wisdom that does not lead to God. The world says things that sound wise but does not lead to God.

When pastors have yielded themselves and become conformed to this world, their preaching is filled with wise sounding sayings and mental delights that do not yield spiritual fruits. People hail such preachers as wise men because when they speak it sounds like the audio version of *Encyclopaedia Britannica.*

There is no need to yield yourself to the worldly way of thinking. Do not pride yourself in having read the biographies of President Bill Clinton, President Barrack Obama, President François Mitterand, Winston Churchill, Lee Kuan Yew and Margaret Thatcher instead of having read the biographies of William Carey, Adoniram Judson, Oral Roberts or Kenneth Hagin. The people you admire and the books you read reveal how much your thinking has been conformed to this world.

One day, I met a brother who was more influenced by secular things than the Bible. I encouraged him to play golf because Yonggi Cho and other pastors I knew had developed that habit for health and other good reasons. However, I could not convince him to learn how to play golf so I decided to give him the biography of Lee Kuan Yew. When he read how Lee Kuan Yew was an avid golfer, he decided to play golf. Clearly, this fellow was more influenced by secular thinking than by biblical and spiritual things. Do not become someone whose mind is conformed to the thinking of this world. We are not of those who speak the wisdom of this world.

The world has a way of thinking when it comes to financial things. The world believes in bonds, debts, mortgages, loans, financial engineering, hire purchase agreements, negotiated funding, credits, hedging and so on. Today, the richest countries in the world are laden with debt and many people who claim to be prospering are deeply in debt. There is nothing real about their prosperity because of the worldly wisdom and systems that they have adopted.

The word of God gives a different kind of wisdom when it comes to financial things. The wisdom of the Word may not have such high-sounding words but it is still the wisdom of God. God, in His word, teaches against loans and borrowing.

> For the LORD thy God blesseth thee, as he promised thee: and thou shalt lend unto many nations, BUT THOU SHALT NOT BORROW; AND THOU SHALT REIGN over many nations, but they shall not reign over thee.
>
> Deuteronomy 15:6

Through the Bible you see how God directs you away from borrowing, no matter the name given to it. It shows that you shall reign over nations and no one will reign over you if you walk in the responsibility and blessing of not borrowing.

CHAPTER 5

Overcome the Pressure to Love this World

LOVE NOT THE WORLD, NEITHER THE THINGS THAT ARE IN THE WORLD. If any man love the world, the love of the Father is not in him. For all that is in the world, the lust of the flesh, and the lust of the eyes, and the pride of life, is not of the Father, but is of the world.

1 John 2:15-16

Do not love the world, my brother! Loving this world is a dangerous spiritual mistake. Demas made this terrible mistake and abandoned the ministry.

> For Demas hath forsaken me, HAVING LOVED THIS PRESENT WORLD, and is departed unto Thessalonica; Crescens to Galatia, Titus unto Dalmatia.
>
> 2 Timothy 4:10

Why is it so wrong for a Christian fall in love with the world? It is wrong because the world you are in is your mission field. You have been sent into the world as an ambassador of Christ. Imagine if the American Ambassador who is sent to China falls in love with China and after four years adopts all the ideas and philosophies of China that are against America! What about if this American Ambassador becomes more Chinese than he is American? What about if he falls in love with Chinese food, Chinese culture, Chinese language, Chinese ways and Chinese politics?

What about if he begins to dislike the American language, the American culture, the American food and America's democratic political system? Would he be a good ambassador for the United States? Certainly not!

Such an ambassador would be a failed missionary because he has fallen in love with the Chinese world that he was sent to help. Although it sounds absurd, that is exactly what Christians do today. Jesus has sent them into the world and they have fallen in love with the world! Remember Jesus said:

> **" Then said Jesus to them again, Peace be unto you: as my Father hath sent me, EVEN SO SEND I YOU.**
>
> **John 20:21**

How unfortunate it is for Jesus to send us into the world and for us to fall in love with the world that He sent us to save and to preach to! Instead of winning the lost and having compassion for the souls that do not know about God, we have decided to buy shops, invest in farms, buy taxis and settle down in this world forever.

What does it look like when you have forgotten completely about the country that sent you? What is it like when you have been converted by the country that you were sent to convert! That is a tragedy of tragedies!

This is what has happened to the church. Do not love the world! The world is not a place to love! The world is a place to save and have compassion for! The world is not a place to admire! The world is a group of people you must pity and help to be saved!

Signs that You Have Fallen in Love with the World

You can tell whether you are in love with the world or not by looking at the signs that you have when you fall in love with someone. Let us look at the signs that you are in love with someone.

1. **When you are in love with the world, you cannot stop staring at the things that are in the world and admiring them!** When you are in love with a boy, you cannot stop staring at him and admiring him. You admire the riches, the silver the gold, the cars, aeroplanes and houses of this world and stare at them longingly.

2. **When you are in love with the world, you abandon your spiritual activities and follow the world to engage in worldly activities!** When you are in love with a girl, you abandon your usual activities and follow her around.

   Instead of going to church, you attend debating club meetings. Instead of going to church, you attend International Students meetings. Instead of attending prayer meetings, you attend Old Boys' Association meetings. Instead of going to church, you go for lunches, breakfasts and dinners.

3. **When you are in love with the world, you do not mind when the world does things that are obviously wrong!** When you are in love with someone, you do not mind when he does something that is obviously wrong.

   If you love the world, you do not mind when the world does things that are obviously wrong. When the world is accepting sexual perversions, you will not find anything wrong with it. You love the clothes that are too short and simply unacceptable. You consider the worldly clothes as decent clothing. You love the ways of the world!

4. **When you are in love with the world, you accept everything that the world has to offer!** When you are in love with a boy, you are accepting of everything about him. When you are in love with somebody, the person can do no wrong.

   When you are in love with the world, you swallow all the nonsense and deception of the world and you find it acceptable. When you are in love with the world, the ways of the world are always right to you!

5. **When you are in love with the world, you always think about the world and what you can achieve with the world!** Instead of thinking of what you can achieve for God, you are thinking about what worldly achievements you can attain to. You are always thinking of getting more degrees rather than becoming a shepherd or a pastor. You are thinking of getting a better job in the world rather than how you can be a better shepherd.

6. **When you are in love with the world, you want to be accepted in the world, to please the world and to make the world happy!** When you are in love with a girl, you always think about her and you want to make her happy!

   Your desire to be accepted by the world is a sign that you are in love with the world. Your aversion to being the odd-one-out in the world is a sign that you are in love with the world.

CHAPTER 6

Overcome the Pressure to Befriend this World

Ye adulterers and adulteresses, know ye not that THE FRIENDSHIP OF THE WORLD is enmity with God? Whosoever therefore will be a friend of the world is the enemy of God.

James 4:4 (NASB)

There are no meaningless relationships in the world; every single relationship you have has significance, importance and consequence!

Today God is telling you "do not befriend the world". Friendship with the world means something. Friendship with the world has some significance, importance and consequence. Relationships have meanings! There are no meaningless relationships in the world. If you have a relationship with someone, it automatically means that certain other relationships are not going to work.

Friendship with your past boyfriend means your relationship with your husband will be bad. Friendship with your past girlfriend means that your relationship with your wife will be sour. This is the principle that the apostle James is speaking of today. Friendship with the world simply means enmity with God! You must never say that a relationship is meaningless. There are no meaningless relationships in the world! Every relationship has significance, importance and consequence!

Signs that You Have a Friendship with the World

The signs that you have a friendship with the world are easy to deduce. By looking at the signs of your friendship with someone, we can easily see whether you have a friendship with the world or not. Let us look at the signs that you have a friendship with the world.

1. **A good friend is someone whose company you enjoy.** Therefore, the fact that you enjoy the company of the world and worldly people is a sign that you are friends with the world.
2. **A good friend is someone you talk to a lot.** I once knew someone who claimed she did not speak much to a certain man. Yet, the man said of her, "She is my good friend." How can you be a good friend who does not talk much with someone? The much talking is the sign of a good

friendship. Your constant talking with worldly people, to secular people and to unbelievers is a sign that the world is your friend.

3. **A good friend is loyal and dependable.** Someone who is a good friend will be faithful to you and never leave you or forsake you. The fact that you do not want to leave the world, leave your worldly friends and leave certain worldly cities is a sign that you are a friend with the world. You are loyal, dependable and faithful to the world; never forsaking them and never leaving them behind.
4. **A good friend laughs with you.** I remember someone who laughed at me and mocked at me behind my back. Yet, this same fellow claimed friendship and love. How can that be? Your friendship with the world is revealed by how relaxed you are with worldly people. You laugh and chat with the wildest of sinners and you are comfortable in their presence. All that is a sign of your friendship with the world.
5. **A good friend doesn't accuse you but comforts you.** The fact that you do not present the gospel to your worldly friends shows that you do trust and believe in their ways. Instead of confronting them and "accusing" them of their need for salvation, you simply flow along with them and comfort them rather than telling them the truth.

CHAPTER 7

Overcome the Pressure from The Hatred of the World

I HAVE GIVEN THEM THY WORD; AND THE WORLD HATH HATED THEM, because they are not of the world, even as I am not of the world.

John 17:14

It is not a nice thing to be hated by someone. Human beings often do whatever they can to make people like them, rather than hate them. It is better to be far away from someone who hates you. Hatred leads to bitter mistreatment, elimination, intense dislike, harm and even murder.

You will always have a problem of being hated by the world. If you have not yet felt the hatred of this world, you are new to this battle. When you see the world attacking your fellow pastor, you may think he is being attacked because he has committed crimes or sins. You will discover with time that attacks from the world have nothing to do with whether you are good or bad. No matter how clean or innocent you are, the hatred of the world will be manifested against those who believe. The world hates Christians and the world hates the church.

> **If you were of the world, the world would love its own; but because you are not of the world, but I chose you out of the world, BECAUSE OF THIS THE WORLD HATES YOU.**
>
> **John 15:19 (NASB)**

Signs that the World Hates You

1. Sign of hatred: non-recognition by the world.

> Behold, what manner of love the Father hath bestowed upon us, that we should be called the sons of God: therefore THE WORLD KNOWETH US NOT, because it knew him not.
>
> 1 John 3:1

You will always have a problem with non-recognition by the world. The world does not recognize Christians. That is why many governments do not recognize the church and its input unless it is politically helpful to do so. The people of this world do not see the importance of the church nor of Christians.

When someone hates you, his body language often reveals it. The body language of the world reveals their hatred for us. When someone hates you, he avoids eye contact with you. The world avoids eye contact with us!

The world does not want to know us! The world dislikes us! The world does not know or understand what we believe in. The world has a negative posture towards the church. Jesus said, "The world knoweth us not." They do not know who we are and they do not recognize us.

2. Sign of hatred: envy.

> For we ourselves also were sometimes foolish, disobedient, deceived, serving divers lusts and pleasures, living in malice and envy, hateful, and hating one another.
>
> Titus 3:3

Envy is a feeling of discontentment at someone else's success, advantage, advancement or happiness. Envy is a manifestation of hatred and ill-will. The world hates believers and so you can expect a feeling of discontentment and ill-will when the church seems to be advancing or successful. The world has a feeling of ill-will towards us when they see that we are happy and serving the Lord. That will always be the case and we must not expect the world to love us.

3. Sign of hatred: humiliation and mistreatment by another person.

> Whosoever hateth his brother is a murderer: and ye know that no murderer hath eternal life abiding in him.
>
> 1 John 3:15

You can expect the world to humiliate and mistreat you if they can. When the world had a chance to touch our Saviour, the entire city of Jerusalem rose up to humiliate and mistreat the One who had preached amongst them, healed their sick and ministered love to them. The open and spontaneous hatred of the world against Jesus Christ when they had the opportunity is a revelation for all ministers of the gospel.

CHAPTER 8

We Have Another World in View

And I saw A NEW HEAVEN AND A NEW EARTH: for the first heaven and the first earth were passed away; and there was no more sea.

Revelation 21:1

We are expecting to arrive in another world very soon. One day, we will not be living here any longer. We will be living in glory with the Lord. Everything we have gathered on this earth will be left behind. Everything we have built on this earth will be left behind. We will be well established in another world.

The entire Bible is filled with scriptures that prove that we have another world in view.

1. **A new world is about to come into existence.** The world that we know will be replaced by another world – the world that is to come! The world in view is the future world.

   Far above all principality, and power, and might, and dominion, and every name that is named, NOT ONLY IN THIS WORLD, BUT ALSO IN THAT WHICH IS TO COME:

   Ephesians 1:21

2. **The future world in view will be different from this present world because the lusts of this world will be gone forever.** When this world passes away, certain desires will pass away forever. This is very good news! You will be disconnected from your current desires. The desires we all have, have driven us away from God.

   And THE WORLD PASSETH AWAY, AND THE LUST THEREOF: but he that doeth the will of God abideth for ever.

   1 John 2:17

3. **The world in view will have some major differences.** There will be no sea or oceans in the new world. Today, the oceans represent a dark, deep, frightening and uncertain place of death for anyone who falls into it. God has decided to do away with the sea in the next world.

God Himself, the presence of God will be with us in the next world. Today, we hardly feel the presence of God with us on any part of the earth. In the new world, you will feel God's presence everywhere. God will wipe the tears from our eyes. At every point in time in this world, someone is crying tears of anguish and tears of regret. Such things will not exist in the new world that is to come.

There will be no more curse in the new world that is to come. The world in view will be far greater than this current world. This current world is not worthy of believers today. So great is the world that is to come! This world is not our home!

> AND I SAW A NEW HEAVEN AND A NEW EARTH: FOR THE FIRST HEAVEN AND THE FIRST EARTH WERE PASSED AWAY; and there was no more sea.
>
> And I John saw the holy city, new Jerusalem, coming down from God out of heaven, prepared as a bride adorned for her husband.
>
> And I heard a great voice out of heaven saying, Behold, the tabernacle of God is with men, and he will dwell with them, and they shall be his people, and God himself shall be with them, and be their God.
>
> And God shall wipe away all tears from their eyes; and there shall be no more death, neither sorrow, nor crying, neither shall there be any more pain: for the former things are passed away.
>
> And he that sat upon the throne said, Behold, I make all things new. And he said unto me, Write: for these words are true and faithful.
>
> Revelation 21:1-5

> And he shewed me a pure river of water of life, clear as crystal, proceeding out of the throne of God and of the Lamb.
>
> In the midst of the street of it, and on either side of the river, was there the tree of life, which bare twelve manner of fruits, and yielded her fruit every month: and the leaves

of the tree were for the healing of the nations.

AND THERE SHALL BE NO MORE CURSE: but the throne of God and of the Lamb shall be in it; and his servants shall serve him:

Revelation 22:1-3

4. **The future world will have the kingdoms of our Lord replacing the kingdoms of this world.** That is when the saying that "the kingdoms of this world have become the kingdoms of his Christ" will come to pass. The kingdoms of this world were handed over to satan and since then he has been the god of this world. Jesus Christ came to destroy the power of the god of this world and to set many people free. "And the devil said unto him, All this power will I give thee, and the glory of them: for that is delivered unto me; and to whomsoever I will I give it" (Luke 4:6).

And the seventh angel sounded; and there were great voices in heaven, saying, THE KINGDOMS OF THIS WORLD ARE BECOME THE KINGDOMS OF OUR LORD, and of his Christ; and he shall reign for ever and ever.

Revelation 11:15

5. **The future world will have people like you as the rulers.** People we know as nobodies on earth will become presidents and heads of states of the nations. We will become the rulers of the world in view.

And unto one he gave five talents, to another two, and to another one; to every man according to his several ability; and straightway took his journey.

Then he that had received the five talents went and traded with the same, and made them other five talents.

And likewise he that had received two, he also gained other two.

But he that had received one went and digged in the earth, and hid his lord's money.

After a long time the lord of those servants cometh, and reckoneth with them.

And so he that had received five talents came and brought other five talents, saying, Lord, thou deliveredst unto me five talents: behold, I have gained beside them five talents more.

His lord said unto him, Well done, thou good and faithful servant: thou hast been faithful over a few things, I WILL MAKE THEE RULER over many things: enter thou into the joy of thy lord

Matthew 25:15-21

6. **The future world will not have angels in charge of it.** The future world will have human beings like us in charge.

FOR UNTO THE ANGELS HATH HE NOT PUT IN SUBJECTION THE WORLD TO COME, whereof we speak.

But one in a certain place testified, saying, what is man, that thou art mindful of him? Or the son of man, that thou visitest him?

Thou madest him a little lower than the angels; thou crownedst him with glory and honour, and didst set him over the works of thy hands:

Thou hast put all things in subjection under his feet. For in that he put all in subjection under him, he left nothing that is not put under him. But now we see not yet all things put under him.

Hebrews 2:5-8

7. **The world in view will have new and wonderful powers.** You will be one of those who will use the powers of the world to come. Perhaps there will be wonderful powers

that can make you fly or appear anywhere you want to. I am excited about the world in view. I hope you are excited too. It will be nice to use the supernatural and superior powers of the world to come.

And have tasted the good word of God, and the POWERS OF THE WORLD TO COME,

Hebrews 6:5

CHAPTER 9

Accept to be a Fool in this World

Howbeit we speak wisdom among them that are perfect: YET NOT THE WISDOM OF THIS WORLD, nor of the princes of this world, that come to nought: But we speak the wisdom of God in a mystery, even the hidden wisdom, which God ordained before the world unto our glory: Which none of the princes of this world knew: for had they known it, they would not have crucified the Lord of glory. But as it is written, Eye hath not seen, nor ear heard, neither have entered into the heart of man, the things which God hath prepared for them that love him.

1 Corinthians 2:6-9

God expects us to live in this world and apply the rules of *another* world, and "not the wisdom of *this* world"! God considers the wisdom of this world to be foolishness. He expects us *not* to apply the wisdom of this world in this world. We have another world in view! Although we live in this world we are not of this world.

We are living by faith in this world and expecting to overcome through the wisdom of God. We will receive things that eye has not seen and ear has not heard if we walk with the wisdom of God whilst in this world. If we can learn to avoid the wisdom and thinking of this world, we will see great things that we never imagined.

We have another world in view! Although we live in this world, our eyes are set on a world that is coming soon. Every believer must have another world in view. Without having another world in view, you will not be able to reject the wisdom of this world. The wisdom of God will prepare you for the eternal world that is going to descend on us all very soon.

> **Let no man deceive himself. IF ANY MAN AMONG YOU SEEMETH TO BE WISE IN THIS WORLD, LET HIM BECOME A FOOL, THAT HE MAY BE WISE.**
>
> **For the wisdom of this world is foolishness with God. For it is written, He taketh the wise in their own craftiness.**
>
> **1 Corinthians 3:18-19**

We are supposed to become fools in this world so that eventually, we will be wise. As far as this world is concerned, you are supposed to be a fool. The way you live your life as a good Christian will make people mock you. There is one reason why you must decide to become a fool in this world. *The reason why you will be a fool in this world is because you will be applying the wisdom from another world.*

When you are in a country, you must live by the rules of that country otherwise you will become a fool. We are considered as fools because we have another world in view and we live by the rules of that other world.

The wisdom of this world says, "Get all you can and store it up for a rainy day." But the wisdom of God says, "Give and it shall be given unto you, good measure, pressed down, shaken together and running over" (Luke 6:38).

The wisdom of this world says, "If you want to go higher and be promoted, work hard and pull down everything that is ahead of you and that seems to block your path." But the wisdom of God says, if you want to go higher, go lower. Humble yourself in the sight of God and He will lift you up! (James 4:10).

I was once in a country that had some strange rules that everyone lived by. I did not understand what they were doing when they applied those rules. However, I came to realise that it was wisdom to live by those rules in that country.

In this particular country, they had evening church services in the afternoon. I could not understand why we were going for the evening service in the afternoon. Later on, I found out that it was dangerous to be driving in that city after 9.00 pm. The pastor said to me, "There is no reason on earth for me to be out of my house after 10.00 pm in this city." If I applied the rules of my country in this country, I might find myself becoming a fool and having all sorts of disasters.

On another occasion I was picked up from my hotel and taken to the church to preach. After preaching, I came onto the church car park and walked to the car that had brought me earlier to church. Suddenly, the pastor said, "You cannot go in this car" and he took me to another smaller, much older, dilapidated car. I humbly entered the car and was taken to my hotel. As we were driving, I asked my host why I was brought to the service in a posh car but was being taken back to the hotel in this old jalopy.

He explained, "Over here, you do not drive after 8.00 pm on certain roads in new cars because it is not safe. The car may be stolen from us. It is safer for us to take you back to the hotel in this old car." I realised that the rules that applied in this country were different from the rules that applied in my country. If I applied the rules of my country in this place, I could find myself becoming a fool and having my car stolen. You always become a fool when you apply the rules of one country in another.

Do not be worried if you feel like a fool in this world. Do not be worried if you are applying the rules of another world in this world.

CHAPTER 10

Three Secrets for Living in this World

I am crucified with Christ: nevertheless I live; yet not I, but Christ liveth in me: and the life which I now live in the flesh I live by the faith of the Son of God, who loved me, and gave himself for me.

Galatians 2:20

1. ASSOCIATION WITHOUT CONTAMINATION:

> I pray not that thou shouldest take them out of the world, but that thou shouldest keep them from the evil. THEY ARE NOT OF THE WORLD, EVEN AS I AM NOT OF THE WORLD.
>
> John 17:15-16

Associate without getting contaminated! We have no choice! We have to live in this world and yet not be of the world. There will always be a problem of how to associate with the world without being contaminated by the world. You must learn to stay in this world and yet not be contaminated or stained by the world. Ask the Lord to show you the secret of associating with the world without being contaminated. It takes a delicate, careful balance to associate with the world without contamination.

2. LIVING HERE, SEEKING THERE:

> For all these things do the nations of THE WORLD SEEK AFTER: and your Father knoweth that ye have need of these things. BUT RATHER SEEK YE THE KINGDOM of God; and all these things shall be added unto you.
>
> Luke 12:30-31

Live here and seek there! You will always have a challenge of living in this world and yet seeking your welfare in another world. Even though you live in this world, you are admonished to seek for your welfare in another kingdom. It is like living in Ghana and seeking your welfare in Seoul, Korea.

How to live your life down here on earth without trying to establish a home and to settle down in great prosperity will always be a challenge. "Living here and seeking there" is a challenge for all believers who are in this world. God is giving you the grace to live here and yet to seek there. It is a bit like people living in London who do not build houses in the UK and yet seek and build houses in India because that is where they are originally from.

3. CRUCIFY THE WORLD:

> But God forbid that I should glory, save in the cross of our Lord Jesus Christ, by whom THE WORLD IS CRUCIFIED UNTO ME, and I unto the world.
>
> Galatians 6:14

To crucify the world speaks of bringing a painful, permanent conclusion to your relationship with the world. It is important that you crucify the world to yourself. When Jesus was crucified, they put a painful and permanent end to His presence in Jerusalem. Jesus Christ was cut off from Israel and from this world when He was crucified outside the gates of Jerusalem.

What a permanent and utter separation came between Jesus Christ and this world! His beautiful voice was heard no more. His wonderful sermons were heard no more. His healing touch was felt no more. He was permanently and utterly separated violently from the world.

Today, that is what is expected of you. You are expected to permanently and utterly separate yourself violently from the world. The world will never have access to you, nor will it influence you any longer.

Today, there are very few things that are happening in the world that are attractive to me. The world is crucified to me. I do not like most of the things in this world. God has given me the grace to permanently cut myself off from the world.

All that you need to do is to bring a cataclysmic conclusion to the relationship between you and worldly men, worldly desires, worldly aspirations and worldly achievements. You will not achieve great things for the kingdom, until the world is crucified to you.

CHAPTER 11

Overcome the Pressure of Materialism in this World

And he said unto them, Take heed, and beware of covetousness: for a man's life consisteth not in the abundance of the things which he possesseth.

Luke 12:15

Jesus Christ spoke directly against materialism. Materialism is an evil spirit that comes from the world. Materialism is a pervading influence that has affected the church of Jesus Christ so much that it has quenched the eternity consciousness that is needed to drive us into the Great Commission.

Materialism is an attitude that attaches too much importance to acquiring things. It is an attitude that is in the world, in which your social status is determined by your possessions.

According to the materialistic spirit of the world, your wealth determines your importance and your rank. Materialism is in direct conflict with the values espoused by Jesus Christ. Materialism tends to impress upon us that possessions can provide happiness. But Jesus Christ told us that a man's life does not consist in the abundance of things that he possesses.

There was a time when it was thought that the Great Commission was a thing of the past. That was the reason why the church did not embark on the Great Commission to all nations. Today, no one is standing up and saying, "Do not go into all the world and preach the gospel to every nation."

Today, the reason why the church does not embark on the Great Commission to all nations is the spirit of materialism. Instead of taking up our crosses and setting aside earthly ambitions, men are filled with the unspoken vision of acquiring as much wealth and earthly possessions as possible. This vision has effectively quenched the Great Commission and the all-important work of church planting and evangelism. It is important to wipe out this evil spirit of materialism that wants to come from the world into your life.

The Four Keys to Quench Worldly Materialism

1. You must plan to carry nothing out of this world.

For we brought nothing into this world, and it is certain we can carry nothing out.

1 Timothy 6:7

It must be your vision to carry nothing out of this world. You must work towards this vision, rather than working in the opposite direction of trying to acquire so many things to take out of this world.

You cannot carry anything out of this world any way. You must not live your life as though you will be able to exit this world with several suitcases of possessions.

When people travel to foreign countries, they often buy many things and pack them into suitcases to carry back to their homes. They do this because they know they can carry these suitcases with them on the plane. They can even take extra suitcases with them if they want to.

Unfortunately, our journey out of this world will not be like that. There will be no suitcases. There will not even be hand luggage! You cannot take your land documents and properties with you to heaven. You cannot take any of your clothes. You cannot take any of your jewellery. You cannot take diamonds to heaven.

In fact, you cannot even take your phone with you. The clothes you wear in your coffin may be specially bought for the occasion whilst the many clothes you really own will be back home.

If you plan to take nothing out of this world, you will quench the spirit of materialism. You will not equate having many possessions with success or happiness.

When the spirit of materialism is killed, you will be free to obey the word of God and follow God's instruction of preaching the gospel to the ends of the world.

2. You must recognise the poor people of this world.

> **Hearken, my beloved brethren, HATH NOT GOD CHOSEN THE POOR OF THIS WORLD RICH IN FAITH, and heirs of the kingdom which he hath promised to them that love him?**
>
> **James 2:5**

The poor of the world must be the group you love most because God has chosen the poor of this world to be rich in faith. When you are attracted to the poor, you are attracted to those whom God is also attracted to. God wants to do many things for the poor. God wants to save the poor and heal the poor of this world. "The Spirit of the Lord is upon me because he has anointed me to preach the gospel to the poor" (Luke 4:18).

3. You must not follow the lust of the eyes.

> **For all that is in the world, the lust of the flesh, and the LUST OF THE EYES, and the pride of life, is not of the Father, but is of the world.**
>
> **1 John 2:16**

The lust of the eyes is one of the big problems of our world. Human beings follow the things they see. People are impressed with what they see even when they know there is something evil about it.

Decide not to walk by sight and you will overcome the spirit of materialism. Do not trust things because they look nice. If you can overcome the lust of the eyes, you will do well as a Christian. If you follow things that are nice to the eyes, you are worldly. A worldly person only has his eyes to go by. A spiritual person does not go by what is nice to the eye.

Moses was successful and faithful to God because he did not follow the lust of the eyes. Moses was moved by the invisible. He was not an ordinary person whose eyes and desires were fixed on things he could see in the natural.

> By faith he forsook Egypt, not fearing the wrath of the king: for he endured, as seeing him who is invisible.
>
> Hebrews 11:27

When you overcome the tendency to be moved by the lust of your eyes, you will become a mighty pillar in the house of God.

4. Do not follow the pride of life.

> For all that is in the world, the lust of the flesh, and the lust of the eyes, and THE PRIDE OF LIFE, is not of the Father, but is of the world.
>
> 1 John 2:16

The Bible teaches us, "Mind not high things" (Romans 12:16). When Christians are conscious of high things, high cars, high houses, high wealth, they neglect the poor of the world. Their mind is on high things.

If you mind high things your mind cannot be on the harvest field because the harvest field is made up of poor people. The harvest fields that are white are made up of dangerous places filled with poor, neglected and suffering people.

> Say not ye, There are yet four months, and then cometh harvest? behold, I say unto you, Lift up your eyes, and look on the fields; for they are white already to harvest.
>
> John 4:35

Such people are not the high and mighty of our world. Materialism and wealth-consciousness kills the Great Commission. The great harvest fields of our world are not tourist cities. The great harvest fields of our world are not places that affluent visitors flock to. The great harvest fields of our world are poor, simple towns and villages, like the ones Jesus visited when He was on the earth.

The Great Commission is to the poor of this world. God has chosen the poor of this world to be rich in faith. If your eye is on high things, you will never see the poor people in the harvest fields.

CHAPTER 12

Live Righteously in this World

For the grace of God that bringeth salvation hath appeared to all men, Teaching us that, denying ungodliness and worldly lusts, we should LIVE SOBERLY, RIGHTEOUSLY, AND GODLY, IN THIS PRESENT WORLD;

Titus 2:11-12

Living righteously in this world is the greatest challenge for believers. There is nothing righteous in this world. Evil spirits are not righteous. There are unclean and evil spirits. They make people unclean and evil. Next to devils, human beings are the most evil creatures on the earth! There are few righteous men on the earth today. "As it is written, There is none righteous, no, not one:" (Romans 3:10).

Anyone who tries to live righteously in this world is going against the tide. Yet, without a great effort to live a righteous life, you cannot claim to be a Christian. How can you live righteously in this world? There are six rules to living righteously in this world.

1. You must live soberly in this world.

> **For the grace of God that bringeth salvation hath appeared to all men, Teaching us that, denying ungodliness and worldly lusts, we should LIVE SOBERLY, righteously, and godly, in this present world;**
>
> **Titus 2:11-12**

Soberness is important for righteousness. Soberness speaks of being free from the influence of anything. Many armed robbers and evildoers take drugs to charge themselves up so they can perform their evil deeds. In their sober state they would not be able to commit the atrocious crimes that they do.

Many people have to come under the influence of something to be able to misbehave as they do.

If you are under the influence of alcohol, tobacco, drugs and weed, you must break out of those influences because these substances will never allow you to live righteously in this life.

Another strong influence is the opposite sex. When you are under the strong influence of a boy or a girl you are not likely to live righteously. There is a reason why they say "Love is blind." When people are in love, they seem not to think properly or act properly. Their inability to think or act properly is because they are not sober. The influence they are under makes them unable to live righteously.

2. You must live righteously in this world.

> **For the grace of God that bringeth salvation hath appeared to all men, Teaching us that, denying ungodliness and worldly lusts, we should LIVE soberly, RIGHTEOUSLY, and godly, in this present world;**
>
> **Titus 2:11-12**

Living righteously must be your goal. Righteousness must be your goal because righteousness is the breastplate in your armour. A large part of your defences is your righteousness. If you are able to walk in righteousness, very few of the long-term plans of satan against you will work.

Satan is constantly looking at your breastplate of righteousness to see if there are any gaps or cracks. Even if you do not know what satan's plans are against you, it is important to keep your breastplate of righteousness intact. When you crack open a section of your armour by living in sin, you can rest assured that the demonic powers will fly into that gap and attempt to destroy you.

3. You must live godly in this world.

> **For the grace of God that bringeth salvation hath appeared to all men, Teaching us that, denying ungodliness and worldly lusts, we should LIVE soberly, righteously, and GODLY, IN THIS PRESENT WORLD;**
>
> **Titus 2:11-12**

Godliness is to do everything that God would do. There are many grey areas in our lives. What shall I do next? What is allowed? What is not allowed? To truly overcome and live righteously, God will have to be your great example. What did

God do and what will God do? By looking at God's example, you will find the path of righteousness. God is love! God forgives! God is kind! God is gracious!

Jesus Christ is the perfect image of God. What did Jesus do? Jesus said, "He that hath seen me hath seen the Father" (John 14:9). How did Jesus handle Judas Iscariot? How did Jesus handle Peter? Exactly how God Himself would have handled them!

4. You must condemn the world by your righteousness.

> **By faith Noah, being warned of God of things not seen as yet, moved with fear, prepared an ark to the saving of his house; BY THE WHICH HE CONDEMNED THE WORLD, and became heir of the righteousness which is by faith.**
>
> **Hebrews 11:7**

Your righteousness must have an effect on the world around you. Noah, by his righteousness, condemned the world around him. Noah's righteousness created the perfect contrast and his lifestyle condemned the world. It is said that thousands of people gathered around Noah's ark when the rain started falling.

There were also thousands of animals around the ark. All these people around the ark who could not get in were condemned. They had rejected Noah's preaching and his righteous life and now they were condemned. Only Noah's family was saved from the flood.

5. You must not follow the lust of the flesh.

> **For all that is in the world, the LUST OF THE FLESH, and the lust of the eyes, and the pride of life, is not of the Father, but is of the world.**
>
> **1 John 2:16**

To walk in righteousness, you must keep yourself from the lusts of the flesh. The flesh is filled with unholy desires. The flesh is the first problem of your life because it makes sin easy and natural for you. Holiness and righteousness are unnatural for you. Holiness and righteousness take great effort because the flesh is naturally desirous of wickedness and sin.

Decide to live the life without following the lust of the flesh. Be conscious of your flesh and what it can do. Your flesh can disgrace you and turn you into a wretched shipwreck.

Your flesh is so tuned to evil that the best word to describe you, when you follow your flesh, is "a wretch". One day, a mother was singing a song in her house. She sang, "Amazing grace, how sweet the sound that saved a wretch like me." Her son asked her, "Mama what is a wretch? Are you a wretch?" Indeed, she was a wretch. Everyone who lives in this flesh is a wretch. A wretch is an unfortunate and miserable person.

Be very conscious of your flesh and respect its power to destroy your righteous life on this earth.

6. You must keep yourself unspotted from the world.

> **Pure religion and undefiled before God and the Father is this, To visit the fatherless and widows in their affliction, and TO KEEP HIMSELF UNSPOTTED FROM THE WORLD.**
>
> **James 1:27**

A spot is the smallest touch, the smallest influence and the smallest indication of worldly contact that has been made with you. God does not want even the smallest touch or influence of the world to be on you. To live righteously, you must avoid even the smallest touch of worldliness.

Indeed, the world has "spots" it can put onto you. Can the "spots" of the world be seen on your dressing, your private life, your music, your language, your friends, your sexual life and your conversation? It is time to put away every spot of the world in your life. Living righteously involves staying away from the spots of the world.

CHAPTER 13

Overcome the Afflictions and Tribulations in this World

We are troubled on every side, yet not distressed; we are perplexed, but not in despair; Persecuted, but not forsaken; cast down, but not destroyed; Always bearing about in the body the dying of the Lord Jesus, that the life also of Jesus might be made manifest in our body. For we which live are always delivered unto death for Jesus' sake, that the life also of Jesus might be made manifest in our mortal flesh.

2 Corinthians 4:8-11

1. **You must expect afflictions, troubles and problems in this world.**

These things I have spoken unto you, that in me ye might have peace. IN THE WORLD YE SHALL HAVE TRIBULATION: but be of good cheer; I have overcome the world.

John 16:33

Jesus has promised afflictions and tribulations in this world. It is amazing that our preaching today consists mostly of promises of a good life with many good things. I believe that such emphases are in direct conflict with the words of Jesus. Jesus promises us tribulation, troubles, problems, crises, trials and issues.

Perhaps, the words of Jesus are words that are meant for ministers of the gospel. After all, Jesus was speaking to His disciples when He spoke these words.

Expecting suffering rather than expecting good times is a weapon of defence. You must arm yourself and defend yourself by having *a mind* that you will go through suffering and difficulty.

Forasmuch then as Christ hath suffered for us in the flesh, arm yourselves likewise with the same mind: for he that hath suffered in the flesh hath ceased from sin;

1 Peter 4:1

2. **You must see your afflictions in this world as an accomplishment.**

Be sober, be vigilant; because your adversary the devil, as a roaring lion, walketh about, seeking whom he may devour: Whom resist stedfast in the faith, knowing that THE SAME AFFLICTIONS ARE ACCOMPLISHED IN YOUR BRETHREN THAT ARE IN THE WORLD.

1 Peter 5:8-9

Every trial and tribulation you go through in this world is an accomplishment in God. As you develop in your spiritual life, you will begin to see troubles, afflictions and trials in order to help you attain great heights in ministry.

The sufferings that you have endured and the problems that you have gone through in this life are definitely part of what gives you a high rank in the kingdom. Your afflictions are true spiritual accomplishments.

3. You must hate your own life.

> **He that loveth his life shall lose it; and he that HATETH HIS LIFE IN THIS WORLD shall keep it unto life eternal.**
>
> **John 12:25**

You must expect that your sufferings and afflictions in this world are going to mount up to the extent that you will hate your very existence in this life.

Jesus expects you to hate your life in this world.

That is quite a demand! To hate your life is to dislike your existence upon the earth. The key to hating your life in this world is to have another world in view. The more you understand the brevity and vanity of your life on this earth, the more you will be able to hate your life on the earth and seek the kingdom of God.

As you hate the world you will be able to set aside all that the world has to offer. You will not need to gain the world any longer and lose your soul.

> **For what is a man profited, if he shall gain the whole world, and lose his own soul? Or what shall a man give in exchange for his soul?**
>
> **Matthew 16:26**

CHAPTER 14

Overcome the Pressure from the Cares of the World

For whatsoever is born of God overcometh the world: and this is the victory that overcometh the world, even our faith. Who is he that overcometh the world, but he that believeth that Jesus is the Son of God?

1 John 5:4-5

1. The Cares of the world choke the calling.

He also that received seed among the thorns is he that heareth the word; and THE CARE OF THIS WORLD, and the deceitfulness of riches, CHOKE THE WORD, AND HE BECOMETH UNFRUITFUL.

Matthew 13:22

I consider the cares of this world to be one of the greatest evils in this life. This is because the cares of the world have the potential to choke the word of God and cause you to become an unfruitful person. All the nations of the world are driven by cares and responsibilities. It is these cares and responsibilities that cancel the word of God in a person's life.

The world we live in is evil and will generate work and responsibilities for you as long as you are alive. The work and responsibilities generated by living in this world are actually the cause of unfruitfulness among believers.

The cares of the world are very effective at removing thoughts of God from your mind. The cares of the world are very effective at removing the call of God from your mind. The cares of the world are very effective at removing the word of God from your mind. Only those who gain the mastery over the cares of the world are able to be effective for God.

2. The Cares of the world make you have wrong priorities.

And seek not ye what ye shall eat, or what ye shall drink, neither be ye of doubtful mind.

FOR ALL THESE THINGS DO THE NATIONS OF THE WORLD SEEK AFTER: and your Father knoweth that ye have need of these things.
But rather seek ye the kingdom of God; and all these things shall be added unto you.

Luke 12:29-31

The greatest evils to befall people who come into this world are the cares of this world. I call it a great evil because cares are a well-camouflaged source of wickedness. Cares do not initially seem to be a source of wickedness. The cares of this world are simply presented as responsibilities that we have in this life.

All the nations of the world are driven by these cares and responsibilities. It is these cares and responsibilities that cause a person to have wrong priorities. Your priorities speak of what you must do first and what you must do second. Anything that you do not do first may never be done. That is why Jesus encouraged us to seek the kingdom of God first. Many things that we decide to do later will simply never be done. Be careful that your priorities do not get mixed up because of the cares of this world.

3. The Cares of marriage in this world cancel the calling.

> **But I would have you without carefulness. He that is unmarried careth for the things that belong to the Lord, how he may please the Lord: BUT HE THAT IS MARRIED CARETH FOR THE THINGS THAT ARE OF THE WORLD, how he may please his wife.**
>
> **1 Corinthians 7:32-33**

One of the most notorious cares of this world is the responsibility that comes upon you because of marriage. Marriage creates monumental cares and responsibilities that are not easy to shake off. Many people are not in the ministry because of their marriages. It takes a very strong man to persist and serve God in the ministry in spite of the cares and responsibilities that he has from his wife and children.

Most ministers present a very lovely picture of their marriages. Unfortunately, this picture is sometimes deceptive. Many marriages are trouble spots and sources of great responsibilities that make men unfruitful in God.

The responsibility of being married to one person and looking after the person as well as children dries out the ministry in most people. You have to be an above average man if you are to overcome the cares of this world that are presented to you through marriage. Some of the strongest callings have been set aside because of marriage.

I remember a pastor who preached one Sunday morning and wept almost throughout the entire sermon. He said his wife had left him because he was a travelling minister and she wanted a "normal" husband.

Since he could not be a normal husband, she divorced him and left him desolate. This pastor cried his way through the sermon because he was so emotionally disturbed. The cares of this world had effectively wiped out the ministry of this pastor and turned him into a divorcee. He may be accused for the rest of his life as being unfaithful to his wife.

CHAPTER 15

How Jesus Related with the World

But Jesus did not commit himself unto them, because he knew all men, And needed not that any should testify of man: for he knew what was in man.

John 2:24-25

You must remember that the world is made up of millions of wicked men, millions of evil spirits and thousands of fallen angels, all living together in one space called earth. This mixture of creatures encountered Jesus Christ, the Son of God and the Saviour of the world. Jesus Christ had an amazing experience on earth. He was loved by some but He was rejected by most! The book of John outlines Jesus' experience in this world that lies in such wickedness.

1. **Jesus Christ came into the world intentionally to meet human beings and to interact with them.**

> He came unto his own, and his own received him not.
>
> John 1:11

Jesus' journey to this earth was a necessary but sad event. I am sure He knew that He was coming to wicked people. It was for the sake of a few people who would receive salvation that He came.

Noah built the ark for just eight people. The great effort of building the ark, which took many years, was undertaken just to save eight people.

Jesus came onto His own, but His own received Him not. Jesus came to His own people! He was hopeful, he had faith; but he knew that very few people would respond to His ministry.

Jesus Himself said, "As it was in the days of Noah so shall it be for the coming of the Son of Man". In the days of Noah very few people responded to the warnings. In the days of Jesus, very few people responded to the gospel.

2. **Jesus Christ made the world but the world did not recognize Him.**

> All things were made by him; and without him was not any thing made that was made. …HE WAS IN THE WORLD, and THE WORLD WAS MADE BY HIM, and the world knew him not.
>
> John 1:3, 10

When Jesus came into the world, they simply asked Him, "Who are you?" Who do you think you are? You cannot come from heaven and tell us what to do!"

The world did not recognize Jesus Christ when He came to walk amongst them. They simply did not recognize their Creator. This astonishing failure to recognize the Son of God happened because human beings, under the influence of evil spirits are truly wicked.

3. The world did not receive Him but as many as received Him, He gave power to become sons of God.

> He came unto his own, and his own received him not. But as many as received him, to them gave he power to become the sons of God, even to them that believe on his name:
>
> John 1:11-12

As was expected, the world rejected Jesus Christ. He came to His own but His own did not receive Him. His own country rejected Him. His own family rejected Him. You cannot expect any better behaviour from such a wicked world. However, there were a few people who received Jesus Christ and believed in Him. Those few people who received Jesus Christ were given power to become sons of God.

4. God showed the whole wide world His love by sending Jesus.

> For GOD SO LOVED THE WORLD, that he gave his only begotten Son, that whosoever believeth in him should not perish, but have everlasting life.
>
> John 3:16

This world, full of wicked men and evil spirits, received the greatest gift from our great God. The men of this wicked world quickly rose up and murdered Jesus Christ, the Saviour of the world. Perhaps they did this to confirm that they were truly evil.

In spite of the atrocious sins of the world, Jesus maintained open arms and great love for the people of this world. Human beings were given a chance to repent but Jesus did not preach the gospel to the evil spirits.

5. God did not send Jesus into the world to condemn the world.

> For God sent not his Son into the world to condemn the world; BUT THAT THE WORLD THROUGH HIM MIGHT BE SAVED.
>
> John 3:17

God intended to save the whole world through Jesus Christ. The world was full of wicked men who were expecting condemnation from the Son of God. They waited for Jesus to condemn them, but He never did. Even on the cross, He prayed that they would be forgiven.

Jesus simply did not come to this world to condemn people. It is unfortunate if people thought that Jesus came to condemn them.

6. The world condemned itself.

> And this is the condemnation, that light is come into the world, and men loved darkness rather than light, because their deeds were evil.
>
> John 3:19

Men loved the darkness that they were involved with. They did not want to give up their lives of sin and wickedness. God did not send Jesus to condemn anyone in this world. The condemnation of this world is simply because it did not open its arms to receive the grace of God that had appeared to men.

7. The world hated Jesus Christ.

> THE WORLD CANNOT HATE YOU; BUT ME IT HATETH, because I testify of it, that the works thereof are evil.
>
> John 7:7

The world hated Jesus Christ because He spoke the truth about them. Jesus Christ was hated by the world because Jesus Christ spoke the truth about the world. Today, there are many people who hate you because you tell them the truth. I have encountered people filled with so much hatred just because they were corrected and told the truth about their lives.

8. Jesus is the light of the world.

> Then spake Jesus again unto them, saying, I AM THE LIGHT OF THE WORLD: he that followeth me shall not walk in darkness, but shall have the light of life.
>
> John 8:12

When you follow Jesus, you will not walk in the darkness of this life. There is great darkness in the world today. Following Jesus Christ takes you away from the darkness and evil of this world.

9. Jesus was very happy to go out of this dangerous world.

> And NOW I AM NO MORE IN THE WORLD, BUT THESE ARE IN THE WORLD, and I come to thee. Holy Father, keep through thine own name those whom thou hast given me, that they may be one, as we are.
>
> John 17:11

By the time Jesus was about to be crucified, He knew that He was no longer a part of this world. Even though He was in the world, He was virtually out of the system. There is a time just before death that is the same as death itself.

10. Jesus Christ prayed for His disciples because He had to leave them in a dangerous world.

> And now I am no more in the world, but these are in the world, and I come to thee. Holy Father, keep through thine own name those whom thou hast given me, that they may be one, as we are.
>
> John 17:11

Jesus was happy to leave this world but He was concerned about His disciples. He wanted them to stay united because that way, they would be stronger together against the enemy. The disciples were going to have to take the gospel to millions of wicked and unrepentant men. The disciples were going to have to preach the word of God in spite of the hostility from millions of demons. Demons are very evil creatures who exist to oppose, accuse, tempt and deceive God's servants. Jesus knew that He was leaving His disciples in a very toxic environment. He said to them, " If the world hate you, ye know that it hated me before it hated you" (John 15:18).

CHAPTER 16

Overcome the World through the Holy Spirit

Ye are of God, little children, and have overcome them: because greater is he that is in you, than he that is in the world.

1 John 4:4

1. **The world cannot receive the Holy Spirit.** The Holy Spirit has a unique relationship with the world. He cannot be received by the world. The world cannot receive the gifts and manifestations of the Holy Spirit. The Holy Spirit cannot be a blessing to the world in the way that He is to the church.

If you want to receive the full blessing of the Holy Spirit, you must be a believer. Without being a believer, you cannot experience the gifts, the manifestations, the operations and the administrations of the Holy Spirit in His fullness. Once you are an unbeliever, the Holy Spirit has one ministry towards you. He wants to convict you of sin, righteousness and judgment.

> Even the Spirit of truth; whom THE WORLD CANNOT RECEIVE, because it seeth him not, neither knoweth him: but ye know him; for he dwelleth with you, and shall be in you.
>
> John 14:17

2. **The Holy Spirit is the only one who can convict the world of sin, of righteousness and of judgment.**

> And when he is come, he will REPROVE THE WORLD OF SIN, and of RIGHTEOUSNESS, AND OF JUDGMENT: of sin, because they believe not on me;
>
> John 16:8-9

The first role of the Holy Spirit is to convict the world of sin. The Holy Spirit's principal ministry to the world is to convict the world of sin, of righteousness and of judgment. The world, full of wicked men, has a warped understanding of sin. Men filled with evil spirits do not know when they have committed sins. Right is wrong and wrong is right! Men have become abnormal in their knowledge.

Today, we have people who are calling sin a human right. Sexual perversions are championed by the most dignified and respected heads of state. All these reveal a warped understanding of sin. Without the Holy Spirit, sin is called righteousness.

There are nations today that have passed laws making it illegal to believe in or preach about certain parts of the Bible. Such laws have been made by people who claim to champion human rights, such as the right to believe, the right to have a faith, the right to have a religion, and the right to free speech.

The second role of the Holy Spirit is to convict the world about righteousness. Only the Holy Spirit can reveal what true righteousness is. You will notice that everyone has a different opinion about what is right.

Even information from the Bible can give seemingly conflicting views about what is right, what can be done and what is acceptable. It is the Holy Spirit who convicts the world of righteousness.

The third role of the Holy Spirit is to convict the world of judgment. One of the most amazing things to see is a person who is completely unconcerned about judgments that are piling up against him. He seems not to care about anything.

Such a fellow seems not to notice and seems not to be concerned about judgments coming to him. You may warn him that he is going to hell, but he may smile at you and carry on. This fellow has not been convicted about the reality of judgment. People simply are not bothered by judgments because the Holy Spirit has not convicted them.

The One who convicts people about their judgment is the Holy Spirit. When the Holy Spirit convicts someone about judgment, he will repent and turn away from his sins.

It is important for us to pray for the Holy Spirit so that He will come into our ministries and convict people of sin, righteousness and judgment. Without the Holy Spirit helping us, our preaching is going to fall on deaf ears. The world will never be converted or changed until the Holy Spirit moves and convicts the people of sin, of righteousness and of judgment.

CHAPTER 17

Prepare for the End of the World

The field is the world; the good seed are the children of the kingdom; but the tares are the children of the wicked one; The enemy that sowed them is the devil; the harvest is the end of the world; and the reapers are the angels. As therefore the tares are gathered and burned in the fire; so shall it be in THE END OF THIS WORLD. The Son of man shall send forth his angels, and they shall gather out of his kingdom all things that offend, and them which do iniquity;

Matthew 13:38-41

This world will finally be overcome when God destroys it through judgment. The world as we know it is coming to an end. This toxic environment in which evil men and women, demons, dragons, unclean spirits and fallen angels are all crowded together in one little space is soon going to end. This world has to come to an end! It is too evil! God has always destroyed evil by giving it a shorter lifespan.

When man fell into sin, God shortened the days that he was allowed to live on the earth. This world has fallen into irreparable wickedness. The life on this planet cannot carry on forever. It has to end and Jesus has told us exactly how it will come to an end.

Jesus predicted that the world will come to an end. When the world comes to an end, the balance of power will change. The first will be last and the last will be first! Many things will turn upside down!

At the end of the world, the conditions that will prevail will be conducive for the growth of both good and evil. It is for this reason that Jesus said we should leave the wheat and the tares to grow together.

It is going to be difficult to see the difference between good and evil.

In the last days there is going to be a lot of liberty. Because of this liberty, evil will grow and multiply. Men will be at liberty to be immoral, wicked and to live without boundaries or restrictions. These will cause the harvest of the tares to ripen.

In the same way, the harvest of the wheat will ripen under the environment of end-time liberty. Where the Spirit of the Lord is, there is liberty. Men will walk in the liberty of the Spirit and serve God without restrictions and without inhibitions. This will cause the church and God's kingdom to multiply.

The end of this world will be like the days of Noah. There will be eating and drinking without any concern for spiritual things. The end of this world will also be like the days of Lot when Sodom and Gomorrah were judged for their lewdness and wickedness. We are in the last days. Perhaps we are in the last minutes of the last days. What are the signs of the end of this world which lies in such wickedness?

Twenty Signs of the End of the World

1. Deceptions

> And Jesus answered and said unto them, Take heed that no man DECEIVE YOU. For many shall come in my name, saying, I am Christ; and shall deceive many.
>
> Matthew 24:4-5

> And many false prophets shall rise, and shall deceive many.
>
> Matthew 24:11

> For there shall arise false Christs, and false prophets, and shall shew great signs and wonders; insomuch that, if it were possible, they shall deceive the very elect.
>
> Matthew 24:24

2. False Christs

> For many shall come in my name, saying, I AM CHRIST; and shall deceive many.
>
> Matthew 24:5

> Then if any man shall say unto you, Lo, here is Christ, or there; believe it not.
>
> For there shall arise false Christs, and false prophets, and shall shew great signs and wonders; insomuch that, if it were possible, they shall deceive the very elect.
>
> Behold, I have told you before. Wherefore if they shall say unto you, Behold, he is in the desert; go not forth: behold, he is in the secret chambers; believe it not.
>
> Matthew 24:23-26

3. **Wars and rumours of wars**

And ye shall hear of WARS AND RUMOURS OF WARS: see that ye be not troubled: for all these things must come to pass, but the end is not yet.

Matthew 24:6

4. **Famines**

For nation shall rise against nation, and kingdom against kingdom: and there shall be FAMINES, and pestilences, and earthquakes, in divers places.

Matthew 24:7

5. **Epidemics and pandemics**

For nation shall rise against nation, and kingdom against kingdom: and there shall be famines, and PESTILENCES, and earthquakes, in divers places.

Matthew 24:7

6. **Earthquakes**

For nation shall rise against nation, and kingdom against kingdom: and there shall be famines, and pestilences, and EARTHQUAKES, in divers places.

Matthew 24:7

7. **Anti-Semitism**

Then shall they deliver you up to be afflicted, and shall kill you: and ye shall be hated of all nations for my name's sake.

Matthew 24:9

8. **Offences**

And then shall many be OFFENDED, and shall betray one another, and shall hate one another.

Matthew 24:10

9. Betrayal

> And then shall many be offended, and shall BETRAY one another, and shall hate one another.
>
> Matthew 24:10

10. Hatred

> And then shall many be offended, and shall betray one another, and shall HATE one another.
>
> Matthew 24:10

11. False prophets

> And many FALSE PROPHETS shall rise, and shall deceive many.
>
> Matthew 24:11

> For there shall arise false Christs, and false prophets, and shall shew great signs and wonders; insomuch that, if it were possible, they shall deceive the very elect.
>
> Matthew 24:24

12. Lawlessness

> And because LAWLESSNESS IS INCREASED, most people's love will grow cold.
>
> Matthew 24:12 (NASB)

13. Love decreasing

> And because iniquity shall abound, the love of many shall wax cold.
>
> Matthew 24:12

14. Increased missionary work and evangelism

> And this GOSPEL of the kingdom shall be preached in all the world for a witness unto all nations; and then shall the end come.
>
> Matthew 24:14

15. New Jewish nation

And He will send forth His angels with a great trumpet and they will gather together His elect from the four winds, from one end of the sky to the other.

Matthew 24:31 (NASB)

16. New Jewish temple

When ye therefore shall see the abomination of desolation, spoken of by Daniel the prophet, stand in the holy place, (whoso readeth, let him understand:)

Matthew 24:15

17. Great tribulations

For then shall be GREAT TRIBULATION, such as was not since the beginning of the world to this time, no, nor ever shall be.

Matthew 24:21

18. Flight of Jews from Judea

Then let them which be in Judaea flee into the mountains:

Matthew 24:16

19. Increasing banquets, parties and having fun

For as in the days that were before the flood they were eating and drinking, marrying and giving in marriage, until the day that Noe entered into the ark,

Matthew 24:38

20. Increasing atheism and unbelief.

For the coming of the Son of Man will be just like the days of Noah.

For as in those days which were before the flood they were eating and drinking, they were marrying and giving in marriage, until the day that Noah entered the ark, they did not understand until the flood came and took them all away; so shall the coming of the Son of Man be.

Matthew 24:37-39 (NASB)

Conclusion

Arm yourself with the knowledge of these signs and prepare yourself for the cataclysmic conclusion of this world. Overcome the world and all that it presents. God is giving you the upper hand in your battle against the world. Do not be conformed to this world! Do not love the world! Do not have a friendship with the world! Do not be destroyed by the cares of the world! You have overcome the world! Who is he that overcometh the world? You are the one that overcomes the world today!

To the making of many books there is no end!